This Book Belongs To

....

This edition first published 1998
by Hodder Children's Books
A Division of Hodder Headline plc
338 Euston Road
London NW1 3BH

A catalogue record for this book is available from
the British Library

ISBN 0 340 71665 7

Printed and bound in Great Britain
by The Devonshire Press Ltd., Torquay, Devon TQ2 7NX

Postman Pat ™

and the
Firework Party

John Cunliffe
Illustrated by Stuart Trotter

from the original television
designs by Ivor Wood

Hodder
Children's
Books

a division of Hodder Headline plc

For George,
another lover of bright colours
J.C.

Chapter One

Jam time!

It was autumn in Greendale.
The leaves were falling. The wind
came and made the leaves dance
and whirl. They made leaf-drifts
on roads and paths.

Katy and Tom tried to catch the little spinning wings that fell from the sycamore trees.

They gathered conkers under
the great chestnut trees in the
top field.

Everyone was busy.
Miss Hubbard was making
jam. Her kitchen was full of
baskets of fruit: blackberries,
apples and plums. The jam
pan was bubbling on the stove.

"Mmmmm, that smells good,"
said Pat, as he came up the
garden path with the letters.
"Pop some in your bag," said
Miss Hubbard, "I have plenty.
It's been a good year for fruit."

Dorothy Thompson was
making big jars of pickle and
chutney, and apple jelly.

She had a basket-full ready for
Pat, and put it in his van when
he came with the letters.
"Lovely," said Pat. "Thanks
very much."

At Greendale Farm, the
damsons were ready. They
had been up ladders all week,
picking the fruit.

There were so many damsons
that they could never eat them
all. There was a table at the
gate, with boxes of damsons on
it, and a notice saying:

DAMSONS!
HELP YOURSELF.

So Pat did just that.
"Mmmmm, I just love damson
jam," he said.

Chapter Two

Trouble!

It was the time for fireworks, as well as jam. November 5th was getting near. Bonfire night!

There was a big pile of wood in the field at Greendale Farm, ready for the bonfire, and it would soon be time to get the fireworks.

Mrs Goggins would set them out in the post-office shop, in their coloured boxes. Rockets, pin-wheels, roman candles and wicked-looking bangers!

Julian could not wait. He had been saving up his pocket money for weeks.

"The fireworks should be in on Saturday," Mrs Goggins told Pat, and he told everyone else.

They were all talking about
it at school. It was hard for
them to settle down to lessons
that week.

They painted pictures of
fireworks . . .

. . . and wrote poems about
them.

Mr Pringle told them the story
of Guy Fawkes. But the only
thing they wanted was *fireworks*.
The real thing. Their own lovely
boxes of fireworks, with the excit-
ing smell of gunpowder about
them, and the blue touch-papers,
waiting to be lit.

Then, on Tuesday, Julian found
a packet of sparklers left over
from last year, in the back of a
drawer. Sara had a strict rule:
No playing with matches.
"All right, Mum," said Julian.

Well, he didn't break the rule,
but he just could not resist
those sparklers. He lit one from
the sitting-room fire, when
Sara was busy in the garden.

It was lovely! Jess didn't like it
at all. He hid behind a chair.

Julian waved the sparkler to
make patterns in the air. It
made a lovely firework-smell,
and showers of glowing sparks.
When the sparks died down,
the end of the sparkler was
very hot.

Julian was careful not to touch it. He knew it would burn him if he did. He was going to throw it into the fire, when Jess ran out from his hiding place, and tripped him up! The sparkler flew from his hand, and fell on the carpet!

There was a smell of burning wool. Julian quickly picked the sparkler up, and dropped it in the fire. Then he said,
"Oh, Jess, look!"
There was a black hole in the carpet. When Sara saw it, there would be real trouble!

Julian stood with his foot
covering the hole. But it was
no use. When Sara came in,
she sniffed the air at once,
and said, "What's burning?"
Julian said,
"Ermmmm…"
"Smells like
wool to me,"
said Sara,
"you've not
been…"
"Sorry, Mum,"
said Julian,
beginning
to cry.

"I thought so," said Sara, "the minute I turn my back...come here, let's have a look at you."

Now he had to step away from the hole in the carpet, and Sara said, "Just look at my best carpet! What *have* you been doing?"

Chapter Three

No more fireworks!

Julian was in trouble all right!
Sara was really cross.
"You could have burned the
house down!" she said. "You
are not allowed to play with
matches, you know that."

"Mum," said Julian, "I didn't.
I didn't play with any matches,
honest, I didn't, I just lit it from
the fire. I was ever so careful. It
was Jess, he..."

"Don't you blame poor little
Jess," said Sara.

"No, but he tripped me..."

"It wasn't his fault, poor
little puss,"
said Sara.
"Wait till
your dad
hears about
this."

When Pat came home, Sara told him the whole story. On top of that, he had the *Pencaster Gazette* with him, and there, on the front page, it said:

There was a picture of a house on fire, and the story said that children had been playing with fireworks when a spark had got into the box, and set them all off. Oh dear, that did it.

Sara waved the paper at Julian and Pat, and said,
"That's it, then! No more fireworks in this house."

You could tell that she meant it.
"Not even the sparklers, if Dad
sets them off," said Julian in a
very small voice.
"*No fireworks*," said Sara,
taking up the sparklers, and
putting them in the dustbin.
"Not even if I ..." said Pat.
"*No!*" said Sara.

And that was that.

Chapter Four

Gloom

The other parents in Greendale
agreed with Sara, when they
saw the newspaper. They all
said, "No more fireworks."
When the boxes of fireworks
arrived at the post-office, Mrs
Goggins sent them back.

Oh, what gloom there was at school the next day! There were long faces all round. Mr Pringle did his best to cheer them up. He gave them extra

playtime. He read them funny
poems. He told them about the
school trip to see the lights in
Blackpool. It was no good. They
all looked sad and tearful.

When Pat called in with the letters, the children gathered round him, and said, "Pat, can't we have any fireworks at all? Not ever?"

Pat shook his head, and looked as sad as the children. "I'll see what I can do," he said.

Chapter Five

The Reverend's surprise

When Pat called on the Reverend Timms he told him about the trouble with the fireworks, and how sad the children were.

"Ah," said the Reverend, "I always loved fireworks when I was a boy. But your Sara is quite right, there is nothing as fearful as fire. So dangerous! I once saw a house on fire, oh, yes, it was awful..."

"But what can we do to cheer the children up?" said Pat.

"Hmmm, now let me see," said the Reverend, "what was it that I saw in the *Church News*?

There was something about firework-displays. I know, here it is." He pulled out a magazine from a pile of papers. It said:

AVE A SAFE

FIREWORK PARTY!

"It's about a man in Carlisle,"
said the Reverend, "and he's a
firework expert. He puts on
wonderful firework displays."

"Is it safe?" said Pat.

"Yes," said the Reverend.

"He wears special clothes,
and no one is allowed to get
too near. He even brings his
own fire-engine."

"We could have stalls,"
said Pat.

"And tea and cakes," said
the Reverend.

"Baked potatoes in the fire,"
said Pat.

"Make a real party of it," said
the Reverend.

"Collect money for the church," said Pat.

"And a half share for the hospital," said the Reverend. "I'll phone him this morning."

Chapter Six

Fireworks!

They were in luck. Bill, the
firework man, said he would
be delighted to come and put
on a show.

The Reverend made posters on his computer, and they were in Greendale post-office and the Pencaster shops by Saturday.

Pat told everyone about the Greendale Firework Display as he delivered the letters. The children were smiling again.

They were still picking damsons at Greendale Farm, and Mrs Pottage made a fresh batch of jam, specially for the show.

Alf and Ted put up a big tent
for the stalls and refreshments.

More wood was added to the
bonfire.

More wood was added to the bonfire.

The big day came. Bill arrived
early, with his fire-engine, and
spent all day setting up the

fireworks. He put ropes all
round them, and no one was
allowed near.

A lot of people came from
Pencaster, for a day out. The
jam and cake stalls sold out,
and Mrs Pottage had to send

for fresh supplies of tea and
orange juice. The collecting
boxes filled up with money.

The bonfire was lit at seven o'clock.

"When will the fireworks start?"
said Julian.
"Soon," said Pat.
At that very moment there was a
loud bang, and a shower of
coloured lights spread across the
sky. The crowd said:

Ooooooooh!

It was a wonderful display.
There were rockets, and pin-
wheels and fountains, more
than you could count.

There were bangs and whistles and shrieks to make your ears ring.

And at the very end, when it was time for bed, Bill brought on his fire-engine to give a display. He squirted a huge spout of water over the bonfire, to make sure it was properly out, and everyone cheered.

"That was the best bonfire night ever," said Pat.

"And the safest," said Sara.

"It was great," said Julian. "Just great. Can we have another one, next year?"